NUD... ,
WINK WINK

Nigel Rees

NUDGE NUDGE, WINK WINK

A QUOTEBOOK OF LOVE AND SEX

Illustrated by Willie Rushton

JAVELIN BOOKS
POOLE · NEW YORK · SYDNEY

First published in the UK 1986 by Javelin Books,
Link House, West Street, Poole, Dorset, BH15 1LL

Distributed in the United States by
Sterling Publishing Co., Inc.,
2 Park Avenue, New York, NY 10016

Distributed in Australia by
Capricorn Link (Australia) Pty Ltd,
PO Box 665, Lane Cove, NSW 2066

British Library Cataloguing in Publication Data

Nudge nudge, wink wink: a quotebook of love
and sex.
1. Sex—Quotations, maxims, etc.
I. Rees, Nigel
306.7   PN6084.S49

ISBN 0 7137 1916 8

Cover illustration by Paul Sample

Typeset by Word Perfect 99 Ltd, Bournemouth, Dorset
Printed and bound in Great Britain by Hazell Watson & Viney Ltd
Member of the BPCC Group, Aylesbury, Bucks.

CONTENTS

FOREWORD

I saw it asserted recently that 'apart from sex, politics has undoubtedly inspired more memorable phrases than any other topic'.

This seems to suggest that 'sex' – whatever is meant by that – has been the inspiration for a multitude of quotations.

I decided to investigate whether this was, in fact, the case. *Nudge Nudge, Wink Wink* is the result.

Of the various aspects of love and sexuality that have resulted in quotable remarks, it seems that marriage provides the greatest number. Almost everything that has been said about that institution is unfavourable.

On that subject, as on the others, I must say that, just because I have included quotations in this book, I do not necessarily share or endorse the sentiments expressed in them.

Nevertheless, I am indebted to the numerous speakers and writers quoted in the book – and to the people who drew their remarks to my attention.

N.R.
1986

1

FOREPLAY

Treat every woman as if you have slept with her and you soon will.

Anonymous

Treat a whore like a lady and a lady like a whore.

Wilson Mizner

Make love to every woman you meet; if you get 5 per cent on your outlay, it's a good investment.

Arnold Bennett

Phrase suggested for increasing feminine fervour: You are an A.1 tumble-bun.

John Eichenlaub, M.D., *The Marriage Art*

Have the florist send some roses to Mrs Upjohn and write 'Emily I love you' on the back of the bill.

Groucho Marx, in the film *A Day at the Races,* 1937

To succeed with the opposite sex, tell her you're impotent. She can't wait to disprove it.

Cary Grant, at the age of 72

Never become involved with someone who can make you lose stature if the relationship becomes known . . . sleep *up*.

Aristotle Onassis, quoting his father

Perhaps at fourteen every boy should be in love with some ideal woman to put on a pedestal and worship. As he grows up, of course, he will put her on a pedestal the better to view her legs.

Barry Norman

The girl in the omnibus has one of those faces of marvellous beauty which are seen casually in the streets but never among one's friends. Where do these women come from? Who marries them? Who knows them?

Thomas Hardy

A fellow will remember a lot of things you wouldn't think he remembers. You take me. One day, back in 1896, I was crossing over to Jersey on the ferry, and, as we pulled out, there was another ferry pulling in, and on it there was a girl waiting to get off. A white dress she had on. She was carrying a white parasol. I only saw her for one second. She didn't see me at all, but I'll bet a month hasn't gone by since that I haven't thought of that girl.

Everett Sloane, in the film *Citizen Kane*, script by Orson Welles and Herman J. Mankiewicz

Lolita, light of my life, fire of my loins. My sin, my soul.

Vladimir Nabokov, *Lolita*

The great and terrible step was taken. What else could you expect from a girl so expectant? 'Sex,' said Frank Harris, 'is the gateway to life.' So I went through the gateway in an upper room in the Café Royal.

Edith Bagnold, *Autobiography,* 1969

If you are ever in doubt as to whether or not you should kiss a pretty girl, always give her the benefit of the doubt.

Thomas Carlyle

Men are those creatures with two legs and eight hands.

Jayne Mansfield

Whoever called it necking was a poor judge of anatomy.

Groucho Marx

An inexperienced female kisser: Where do the noses go? I always wondered where the noses would go.

Ernest Hemingway, *For Whom the Bell Tolls,* 1940

On kissing Margaret Thatcher: We have, of course, often done it before, but never on a pavement outside a hotel in Eastbourne. We have done it in various rooms in one way or another at various functions. It is perfectly genuine – and normal and right – so to do.

William Whitelaw, 1975

How can a bishop marry? How can he flirt? The most he can say is: 'I will see you in the vestry after the service.'

Rev. Sydney Smith

These sort of boobies think that people come to balls to do nothing but dance; whereas everyone knows that the real business of a ball is either to look out for a wife, to look after a wife, or to look after somebody else's wife.

R.S. Surtees, *Mr Facey Romford's Hounds,* 1865

Give a man a free hand and he'll run it all over you.

Mae West

N.O.R.W.I.C.H.

Anonymous message between lovers (meaning '(K)Nickers Off Ready When I Come Home')

Manners, please. Tits first.

Traditional foreplay instruction

One more drink and I'd be under the host.

Dorothy Parker

Two people kissing always look like fish.

Andy Warhol

Why don't you come up some time and see me?

Mae West, in the film *She Done Him Wrong,* 1933

I'll come and make love to you at five o'clock. If I'm late, start without me.

Tallulah Bankhead, quoted in Ted Morgan's *Somerset Maugham*

About to exchange her fur wrap for a dressing gown: Would you be shocked if I put on something more comfortable?

Jean Harlow, in the film *Hell's Angels,* 1930

When the Prince de Joinville asked, 'Where? When? How much?':
Your place. Tonight. Free.

Mlle Rachel, eighteenth-century actress

Is that a pistol in your pocket or are you just pleased to see me?

Mae West

Condoms should be marketed in three sizes, because failures
tend to occur at the extreme ends of the scale. . . . We should
package them in different sizes and maybe label them like
olives — jumbo, colossal, and supercolossal — so that men
don't have to go in and ask for the small.

Barbara Seaman, in evidence to a Select Committee on Population, 1978

When a young man said he was six feet seven inches: Never mind
the six feet. Let's talk about the seven inches.

Mae West

In the wilds: It's so quiet up here you can hear a mouse get a
hard-on.

John Belushi, in the film *Continental Divide*, 1981, script by Lawrence
Kasdan

2

SEX REARS ITS UGLY HEAD

The thing that takes the least amount of time and causes the most amount of trouble is Sex.

John Barrymore

Sex is all right but it's not as good as the real thing.

Graffito

Sex is the biggest nothing of all time.

Andy Warhol

I'd rather have a cup of tea than go to bed with someone – any day.

Boy George, 1983

Sex is the last refuge of the miserable.

Quentin Crisp

The big difference between sex for money and sex for free is that sex for money usually costs a lot less.

Brendan Francis

No sex is better than bad sex.

Germaine Greer

Sex is just one damp thing after another.

Graffito

Is sex dirty? Only when it is being done right.

Woody Allen, in the film *Everything You Always Wanted to Know About Sex*, 1972

Sex is like money — very nice to have but vulgar to talk about.

Tonia Berg, 1971

Sex is bad for one — but it's very good for two.

Graffito

After sex: Fun? That was the most fun I ever had without laughing.

Woody Allen, as 'Alvy Singer' in the film *Annie Hall* (1977) (written with Marshall Brickman)

Other vice may be nice, but sex won't rot your teeth.

Graffito

Never miss a chance to have sex or appear on television.

Gore Vidal

Sex is 90 per cent in the head.

Germaine Greer

The idea of using censors to bar thoughts of sex is dangerous. A person without sex thoughts is abnormal.

Justice William O. Douglas, of the US Supreme Court

Among men, sex sometimes results in intimacy; among women, intimacy sometimes results in sex.

Barbara Cartland

Morality in sexual relations, when it is free from superstition, consists essentially of respect for the other person, and unwillingness to use the person solely as means of personal gratification, without regard to his or her desires.

Bertrand Russell, *Marriage and Morals,* 1929

Lovers don't snore.

Joan Hitchcock

Sex – the poor man's polo.

Clifford Odets

A little incompatibility is the spice of life, particularly if he has income and she is pattable.

Ogden Nash

Sex in marriage is like medicine. Three times a day for the first week. Then once a day for another week. Then once every three or four days until the condition clears up.

Peter de Vries

I kissed my first woman and smoked my first cigarette on the same day; I never had time for tobacco since.

Arturo Toscanini

My dad told me, 'Anything worth having is worth waiting for.' I waited until I was fifteen.

Zsa Zsa Gabor

Would you, my dear young friends, like to be inside with the five wise virgins or outside, alone and in the dark, with the five foolish ones?

Dr Montagu Butler, in a sermon at Trinity College chapel, Cambridge, quoted in Edward Marsh's *Ambrosia and Small Beer*

I'm always looking for meaningful one-night stands.
  Dudley Moore

If I had no duties, and no reference to futurity, I would spend my life in driving briskly in a post-chaise with a pretty woman.

Dr Samuel Johnson

When I was young, I used to have successes with women because I was young. Now I have successes with women because I am old. Middle age was the hardest part.

Artur Rubinstein

He had heard that one is permitted a certain latitude with widows, and went in for the whole 180 degrees.

George Ade

I consider a day in which I make love only once virtually wasted.

Porfirio Rubirosa

I like naked ladies – one at a time, in private.

Bernard Levin, 1985

I tend to believe that cricket is the greatest thing that God ever created on earth . . . certainly greater than sex, although sex isn't too bad either. But everyone knows which comes first when it's a question of cricket or sex – all discerning people recognise that. Anyway, don't forget one doesn't have to do two things at the same time. You can either have sex before cricket or after cricket – the fundamental fact is that cricket must be there at the centre of things.

Harold Pinter, interviewed in the *Observer*, 5 October 1980

Advice to his son on sex: The pleasure is momentary, the position ridiculous, and the expense damnable.

The 4th Earl of Chesterfield

3

THE SINGLE LIFE

I am that twentieth-century failure: a happy, undersexed celibate.

Denise Coffey, quoted in the *News of the World*

Lord give me chastity — but not yet.

St. Augustine

Chastity is its own punishment.

Graffito

Nature abhors a virgin — a frozen asset.

Clare Boothe Luce

It is one of the superstitions of the human mind to have imagined that virginity could be a virtue.

Voltaire

Chastity is the most unnatural of the sexual perversions.

Rémy de Gourmont

Virginity is like a balloon — one prick and it's gone.

Graffito

Celibacy is not an inherited characteristic.

Graffito

Those who choose matrimony do well, and those who choose virginity or voluntary abstinence do better.

Pope John Paul II, 1982

Marriage has many pains, but celibacy has no pleasures.

Dr Samuel Johnson

About the only thing you should be able to say about a Catholic priest is that his father wasn't one.

Anonymous

Marriage may often be a stormy lake, but celibacy is almost a muddy horse-pond.

Thomas Love Peacock, *Melincourt,* 1817

It is better to marry than to burn.

1 Corinthians, 7:9

A bachelor lives like a king and dies like a beggar.

L.S. Lowry

On having children: Life is pleasant, but I have no yearning to clutter up the universe after it is over.

H.L. Mencken

When you've got over the disgrace of the single life, it's more airy.

Anonymous Irish woman, quoted by Joyce Grenfell

Bachelors should be heavily taxed; it is not fair that some men should be happier than others.

Oscar Wilde

'Home, Sweet Home' must surely have been written by a bachelor.

Samuel Butler

Bachelors know more about women than married men. If they did not they would be married too.

Johann Wolfgang von Goethe

Honey, I'm single because I was born that way. I never married, because I would have had to give up my favourite hobby – men.

Mae West

I'm not going to make the same mistake once.

Warren Beatty

By persistently remaining single, a man converts himself into a permanent public temptation.

Oscar Wilde

A bachelor never quite gets over the idea that he is a thing of beauty and a boy forever.

Helen Rowland

A bachelor gets tangled up with a lot of women in order to avoid getting tied to one.

Helen Rowland

Why buy a book when you can borrow one from the library?

Anonymous

4

GAY'S THE WORD

Buggery is now almost grown as common among our gallants as in Italy, and . . . the very pages of the town begin to complain of their masters for it. But blessed be God, I do not to this day know what is the meaning of this sin, nor which is the agent nor which the patient.

Samuel Pepys, in his diary, 1 July 1663

This sort of thing [homosexuality] may be tolerated by the French — but we are British, thank God.

Viscount Montgomery, in a House of Lords speech, 26 May 1965

On a homosexual affair between two actors: I don't care what people do, as long as they don't do it in the street and frighten the horses.

Mrs Patrick Campbell

A far from whole-hearted devotion to the pursuit of girls had sometimes struck him as a kind of selection-board requirement for writers and artists. (Musicians showed up in a different light whenever they were sober enough.)

Kingsley Amis, *I Like it Here*

Why did He not marry? Could the answer be that Jesus was not by nature the marrying sort?

Hugh Montefiore, when Vicar of St Mary's, Cambridge, 1967

If God had meant to have homosexuals, he'd have created Adam and Bruce.

Anita Bryant, 1977

Bisexuality immediately doubles your chances for a date on Saturday night.

Woody Allen, 1975

When asked whether the first person he had ever slept with was male or female: I was far too polite to ask.

Gore Vidal

I became one of the stately homos of England.

Quentin Crisp, *The Naked Civil Servant,* 1968

I am the Love that dare not speak its name.

Lord Alfred Douglas, *Two Loves*

I belong to the fag-end of Victorian liberalism.

E.M. Forster, in a broadcast talk, 1946

When asked by a military tribunal in the First World War what he would do if a German tried to rape his sister: I would try to get between them.

Lytton Strachey

When it was rumoured that he was to marry Violet Trefusis, the friend of Vita Sackville-West and Virginia Woolf: Lord Berners has left Lesbos for the Isle of Man.

Lord Berners, in a newspaper notice of his travels

On Vita Sackville-West, who tended to dress in twinset and pearls, with gaiters: She looked like Lady Chatterley above the waist and the gamekeeper below.

Cyril Connolly

Why are women included when surely it is impossible for them?

Queen Victoria, on Section XI of the Criminal Law Amendment Act, 1886. (Originally this outlawed indecency between males and between females in public or private. When the text was shown to Queen Victoria, no one had the nerve to answer her query)

Many years ago I chased a woman for almost two years, only to discover her tastes were exactly like mine: we were both crazy about girls.

Groucho Marx

In the forties, to get a girl you had to be a G.I. or a jock. In the fifties, to get a girl you had to be Jewish. In the sixties, to get a girl you had to be black. In the seventies, to get a girl you've got to be a girl.

Mort Sahl

5

THE FEMALE OF THE SPECIES

There are only two types of women – goddesses and doormats.

Pablo Picasso

Prostitutes for pleasure, concubines for service, wives for breeding.

Sir Richard Burton, quoting Demosthenes ('and a melon for ecstasy' is sometimes added . . .)

On the difference between a diplomat and a lady: When a diplomat says yes, he means perhaps. When he says perhaps he means no. When he says no, he is not a diplomat. When a lady says no, she means perhaps. When she says perhaps, she means yes. But when she says yes, she is no lady.

Prince Otto von Bismarck (attrib.)

You see an awful lot of smart guys with dumb women, but you hardly ever see a smart woman with a dumb guy.

Erica Jong

I married beneath me. All women do.

Lady (Nancy) Astor, in a speech, Oldham, 1951

Why does a woman work ten years to change a man's habits and then complain that he's not the man she married?

Barbra Streisand

Behind every successful man you'll find a woman who has nothing to wear.

James Stewart

As usual there's a great woman behind every idiot.

John Lennon

Women were born without a sense of humour — so they could love men and not laugh at them.

Graffito

When women kiss, it always reminds me of prize-fighters shaking hands.

H.L. Mencken

Women are a problem, but if you haven't already guessed, they're the kind of problem I enjoy wrestling with.

Warren Beatty

The more I see of men the less I like them; if I could but say so of women too, all would be well.

Arthur Schopenhauer

God created women because He couldn't teach sheep how to type.

Ward Hoffman

No woman is worth the loss of a night's sleep.

Sir Thomas Beecham

A woman is only a woman, but a good cigar is a smoke.

Rudyard Kipling

I like the whisky old and the women young.

Errol Flynn

A woman's place is in the wrong.

James Thurber

He that has a white horse, and a fair woman, is never without trouble.

Italian proverb

Brigands demand your money or your life; women require both.

Samuel Butler

There is no greater fan of the opposite sex, and I have the bills to prove it.

Alan Jay Lerner

It's the fallen women who are usually picked up.

Woody Allen, 1973

It's the good girls who keep the diaries; the bad girls never have the time.

Tallulah Bankhead

How do girls get minks? The same way minks get minks.

Graffito

The happiest women, like the happiest nations, have no history.

George Eliot

What most men desire is a virgin who is a whore.

Edward Dahlberg, 'On Lust', *Reasons of the Heart,* 1965

Older women are best because they always think they may be doing it for the last time.

Ian Fleming, quoted in John Pearson's *The Life of Ian Fleming,* 1966

6

THE LIFE IN MY MEN

Men are beasts, and even beasts don't behave as they do.
Brigitte Bardot

All men are rapists and that's all they are. They rape us with their eyes, their laws and their codes.
Marilyn French, *The Women's Room*

All men are like Arabs.
Catherine Deneuve

Bigamy is having one husband too many. Monogamy is the same.
Anonymous

The more I see of men, the more I admire dogs.
Mme de Sévigné

Women like the simpler things in life — like men.
Graffito

I like men to behave like men — strong and childish.
Françoise Sagan

A woman without a man is like a garden without a fence.
German proverb

We made civilisation in order to impress our girl friends.
Orson Welles

If God considered woman a helpmeet for men, He must have had a very poor opinion of man.

Samuel Butler

Love is man's delusion that one woman differs from another – still, man is better off than women; he marries later and dies sooner.

H.L. Mencken

All men are different, but husbands are all alike.

William Howard Taft, *Our Chief Magistrate and His Powers,* 1916

There's simply no other way for a man to feel his manliness, his kingliness if you will, than to be loved by a beautiful woman.

Tony Curtis, 1979

Men who do not make advances to women are apt to become victims to women who make advances to them.

Walter Bagehot

A hard man is good to find.

Mae West

A man with an erection is in no need of advice.

Italian proverb

Macho does not prove mucho.

Zsa Zsa Gabor

It's not the men in my life, but the life in my men that counts.

Mae West

Men who aren't pet-lovers aren't any good in bed.

Jilly Cooper, in TV programme *Good Companions*, 1985

You know more about a man in one night in bed than you do in months of conversation. In the sack, they can't cheat.

Edith Piaf

I like him and it in that order.

Graffito (female)

7

WHATEVER 'IN LOVE' MEANS

Amor vincit omnia (Love conquers all).
  Virgil

When asked if he was in love on getting engaged to Lady Diana Spencer: Yes — whatever 'in love' means.
  Prince Charles, 1981

If love is the answer, can you rephrase the question?
  Lily Tomlin

Any time that is not spent on love is wasted.
  Tasso

When people say, 'You're breaking my heart,' they do in fact usually mean that you're breaking their genitals.
  Jeffrey Bernard, 1985

Love is not altogether a delirium, yet it has many points in common therewith.
  Thomas Carlyle

The Art of Love: knowing how to combine the temperament of a vampire with the discretion of an anemone.
  E. Michel Cioran

Love is the delightful interval between meeting a beautiful girl and discovering that she looks like a haddock.

John Barrymore

Love is being stupid together.
  Paul Valéry

Love is the triumph of imagination over intelligence.
  H.L. Mencken

Love means not ever having to say you're sorry.
  Erich Segal, *Love Story,* 1970

When a person is in love, he doesn't care about Biafra.
  Françoise Sagan, 1981

Nothing is better for the spirit or body than a love affair. It elevates thoughts and flattens stomachs.
  Barbara Howar, *Laughing All the Way,* 1973

Love is like the measles; we all have to go through it.
  Jerome K. Jerome

I have fallen in love with all sorts of girls and I fully intend to go on doing so.
  Prince Charles, 1975

I went out bicycling one afternoon, and suddenly, as I was riding along a country road, I realised that I no longer loved Alys.
  Bertrand Russell, *Autobiography*

With these few words I want to assure you that I love you and if you had been a woman I would have considered marrying you, although your head is full of grey hairs, but as you are a man that possibility doesn't arise.

Idi Amin, to President Nyerere of Tanzania, August 1972

Love is so much better when you are not married.

Maria Callas

One should always be in love. That is the reason one should never marry.

Oscar Wilde

A lover has all the good points and all the bad points which are lacking in a husband.

Honoré de Balzac, *The Physiology of Marriage,* 1829

The less we love a woman, the more we are loved by her.

Alexander S. Pushkin

There is a codeword which opens safes – it is LOVE.

Anonymous notice in West German Government offices, 1979

Love letters are the campaign promises of the heart.

Robert Friedman

I was in love once when I was young. But then I became attached to the Bureau.

J. Edgar Hoover, director of the FBI, 1924–72

You can always get someone to love you – even if you have to do it yourself.

Thomas L. Masson

To love oneself is the beginning of a lifelong romance.

Oscar Wilde

I never loved another person the way I loved myself.

Mae West

To Oscar Levant: If you had it all over again, Oscar, would you fall in love with yourself?

George Gershwin

When people have loved me I have been embarrassed.

W. Somerset Maugham

8

PARTS, FOREIGN

The French boys will be naught. Their minds do chiefly run on the propagation of their race.

John Aubrey, *Brief Lives*

Continental people have sex-life; the English have hot-water bottles.

Georges Mikes, *How To Be an Alien,* 1946

Once they call you a Latin Lover, you're in real trouble. Women expect an Oscar performance in bed.

Marcello Mastroianni

For adult women wishing to marry, the best prospects are in Greenland.

UN division for Economic and Social Information, 1984

Everything short of war, President Roosevelt promised the English by way of help in the dark days of the blitz; in the same way, American girls are liable to promise their beaux everything short of fornication.

Malcolm Muggeridge

Australia: where men are men and sheep are nervous.

Graffito

You just leave those Russians to me, honey. I'll take 'em all on, a battalion at a time, and send them back to Omsk with their little tails between their legs.

Mae West

The Welsh are the only husbands to put their wives on their national flag.

Anonymous

What men call gallantry, and gods adultery, is much more common where the climate's sultry.

Lord Byron

9

WHATEVER TURNS YOU ON

The mind is an erogenous zone.
  David Frost

Were it not for imagination, a man would be as happy in the arms of a chambermaid as of a duchess.
  Dr Samuel Johnson

Sex appeal is 50 per cent what you've got and 50 per cent what people think you've got.
  Sophia Loren

The finest bosom in nature is not so fine as what imagination forms.
  Anonymous

Women fall in love through their ears and men through their eyes.
  Woodrow Wyatt, 1985

Male sexual response is far brisker and more automatic: it is triggered easily by things, like putting a quarter in a vending machine.
  Alex Comfort

All a writer has to do to get a woman is to say he's a writer. It's an aphrodisiac.

Saul Bellow

Diagnosing his success as a 'swinger': Power is the ultimate aphrodisiac.

Henry Kissinger

Hair is another name for sex.

Vidal Sassoon

Being baldpate is an unfailing sex magnet.

Telly Savalas

O, what a peacemaker is a guid weel-nilly pintle! It is the mediator, the guarantee, the umpire, the bond of union, the solemn league and covenant ... the sword of mercy, the philosopher's stone, the horn of plenty, and the Tree of Life between Man and Woman.

Robert Burns

Absinthe makes the parts grow stronger.

Jack Hibberd, *Odyssey of a Prostitute,* 1983

On Caroline of Brunswick's behaviour with the dey (governor) of Algiers: She was happy as the dey was long.

Lord Norbury, 1820

What matters is not the length of the wand, but the magic in the stick.

Anonymous

During one late-night House session, John led me into the shadows [of the US Capitol] and we made love on the marble steps that overlook the monuments.

Rita Jenrette, estranged wife of ex-Congressman John Jenrette, in *Playboy,* April 1981

Instructions for the Best Positions on the Pianoforte.

Colonel Peter Hawker, title of book

There are nine and sixty ways of constructing tribal lays,
And − every − single − one − of − them − is − right!

Rudyard Kipling, *In the Neolithic Age*

Hooray, hooray
The first of May −
Outdoor sex
Begins today.

Anonymous

Oral sex is a matter of taste.

Graffito

When Edwina Currie held aloft a pair of handcuffs at a Tory Party conference: I admit I felt a bat's squeak of desire.

The Earl of Gowrie

Men like long nails − in old movies couples were always scratching each other's backs.

Britt Ekland, 1984

Dancing is wonderful training for girls; it's the first way you learn to guess what a man is going to do before he does it.

Christopher Morley

On dancing: A perpendicular expression of a horizontal desire.
George Bernard Shaw

You know what comes between me and my Calvins? Nothing!
Brooke Shields, in Calvin Klein jeans ads, 1980

To the average male there is seemingly nothing so attractive or so challenging as a reasonably good-looking young mother who is married and *alone*.

Shirley MacLaine

In the past a sexy woman was one who lay on a sofa like an odalisque, smoking a cigarette. Now she is an athletic woman.

Hardy Amies, 1984

Sweaty is sexy.

Farrah Fawcett-Majors

Women never look so well as when one comes in wet and dirty from hunting.

R.S. Surtees, *Mr Sponge's Sporting Tour,* 1853

Long-legged girls are fascinating – built for walking through grass.

Laurie Lee

High heels were invented by a woman who had been kissed on the forehead.

Christopher Morley

Asked whether she dressed for men or women: I dress for women and I undress for men.

Angie Dickinson

Only men who are not interested in women are interested in women's clothes; men who like women never notice what they wear.

Anatole France

A dress makes no sense unless it inspires men to want to take it off you.
Françoise Sagan

No woman [is] so naked as one you can see to be naked underneath her clothes.
Michael Frayn, *Constructions* 1974

Brevity is the soul of lingerie.
Dorothy Parker

The ends justify the jeans.
Graffito

I knew I would like her when I saw how her backside moved under her red satin skirt.
James Hadley Chase, *No Orchids for Miss Blandish*

A curved line is the loveliest distance between two points.
Mae West

The girl had as many curves as a scenic railway.
P.G. Wodehouse

I'm just naturally respectful of pretty girls in tight-fitting sweaters.
Jack Paar

On going bra-less: I can't breathe when I'm wearing a brassière.
Jean Harlow

British boobs are the best in the world.
Mrs Jane Contour (sic), bra expert

I was the first woman to burn my bra – it took the fire department four days to put it out.

Dolly Parton

If I hadn't had them, I would have had some made.

Dolly Parton

I really wish my bust was smaller.

Samantha Fox, 1986

10

AND SO TO BED

Physical love, forbidden as it was twenty or thirty years ago, has now become boringly obligatory.

Françoise Sagan, 1985

When asked what people do in nude encounter groups: We do people things.

Anonymous Los Angeles woman, quoted by Gay Talese in *Thy Neighbour's Wife*

Lie down! I think I love you.

Graffito

And so to bed.

Samuel Pepys

Amor vincit insomnia.

Anonymous

Don't ever have sex with someone in your office. Wait until you get home.

Anonymous

Clean grass is better than dirty sheets.

Sir John Robertson, on open-air immorality in a Sydney park

It was not the apple on the tree but the pair on the ground that caused the trouble in the garden.

M.D. O'Connor

An erection is like the Theory of Relativity – the more you think about it, the harder it gets.

Graffito

I am happy now that Charles calls on my bedchamber less frequently than of old. As it is, I now endure but two calls a week and when I hear his steps outside my door I lie down on my bed, close my eyes, open my legs and think of England.

Alice, Lady Hillingdon, in her journal, 1912

His Grace returned from the wars today and pleasured me twice in his top-boots.

Sarah, Duchess of Marlborough

The best f***s are always after a good cry.

Anonymous

On the Pope and birth control: He no play-a da game. He no make-a da rules!

Earl Butz

The best contraceptive is a glass of cold water: not before or after, but instead.

Anonymous delegate at International Planned Parenthood Federation conference

I would not like to leave contraception on the long finger too long.

Jack Lynch, Irish Prime Minister, 1971

Love is two minutes fifty-two seconds of squishing noises. It shows your mind isn't clicking right.

Johnny Rotten (Having acquired a new technique, he later revised this to five minutes)

On Sir Walter Raleigh: One time getting one of the Mayds of Honour up against a tree in a Wood . . . who seemed at first boarding to be somewhat fearfull of her Honour, and modest, she cryed, sweet Sir Walter, what doe you me ask? Will you undoe me? Nay, sweet Sir Walter! Sweet Sir Walter! At last, as the danger and the pleasure at the same time grew higher, she cryed in extasey, Swisser Swatter, Swisser Swatter.

John Aubrey

'Pray, my dear,' quoth my mother, 'have you not forgot to wind up the clock?' — 'Good G--!' cried my father, making an exclamation, but taking care to moderate his voice at the same time, — 'Did ever woman, since the creation of the world, interrupt a man with such a silly question?'

Laurence Sterne, *Tristram Shandy*

On the subject of all-in wrestling: If it's all in, why wrestle?

Mae West

Note left for a friend found in flagrante: Called to see you, but you were in.

Karl Miller

I met my love in a graveyard
I did her before we were wed
I laid her on top of the tombstone
We did it to cheer up the dead.

Brendan Behan

Sex is best in the afternoon after coming out of the shower.
Ronald Reagan, 1949

In the afternoon my wife and I had a little quarrel which I reconciled with a flourish. Then she read a sermon in Dr Tillotson to me. It is to be observed that the flourish was performed on the billiard table.

William Byrd, in his diary, 30 July 1710

As I was sipping my Campari on the ground floor I was informed by my charming hostess that I was missing out on a meaningful confrontation upstairs where a former cabinet colleague of the President was 'talking about Uganda'.

Eager, as ever, to learn the latest news from the Dark Continent I rushed upstairs to discover the dusky statesman 'talking about Uganda' in a highly compromising manner to a vivacious former features editor.

Private Eye, 9 March 1973

And so to Mrs Martin and there did what je voudrais avec her, both devante and backward, which is also muy bon plazer.

Samuel Pepys, in his diary, 4 June 1666

The zipless f*** is the purest thing there is. And it is rarer than the unicorn. And I have never had one.

Erica Jong, *Fear of Flying,* 1973

Since most men can't keep it up long enough to fulfil woman's God-given – and soon to be Constitutioned – right to orgasm, the vibrator can take over while the man takes a leak.

Gore Vidal

Explaining to a young friend what two dogs were doing together:
Well, you see, my dear, the doggie in front has suddenly gone blind, and the other one has very kindly offered to push him all the way to St Dunstan's.

Noel Coward

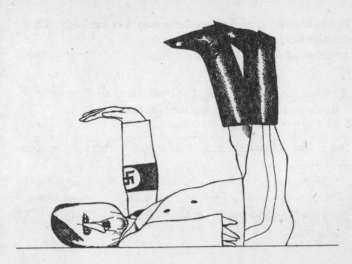

He [Adolf Hitler] doesn't even take his boots off, and sometimes we don't get into the bed. We stretch out on the floor. On the floor he is very erotic.

Eva Braun

They made love as though they were an endangered species.

Peter de Vries

I got married, and we had a baby nine months and ten seconds later.

Jayne Mansfield

I only saw him twice and we have two children.

Sheilah Graham, 1984

A woman is a well-served table that one sees with different eyes before and after the meal.

Honoré de Balzac

Giving reasons for preferring older women: 8th and lastly. They are so grateful!

Benjamin Franklin

After sex: Now I know what I've been faking all these years.

Goldie Hawn, in the film *Private Benjamin*, 1980

Sex is like a bank account — after you withdraw you lose interest.

Graffito

Fifty men outside? I'm tired. Send some of them home.

Mae West

11

SOLITARY PLEASURES

George, the Second Duke of Buckingham, when he was about twenty years old, had at Paris desired Mr Hobbes to read Geometry to him. His Grace had great 'natural parts', and quickness of wit. Master Hobbes read, and his Grace did not apprehend him, which Master Hobbes wondered at. At last, he observed that his Grace was at mastrupation. He had his hand in his codpiece.

John Aubrey, *Brief Lives*

On why her canary was called Onan: Because he spills his seed on the ground.

Dorothy Parker

Masturbation is the thinking man's television.

Christopher Hampton, *The Philanthropist*

Masturbation is coming unscrewed.

Graffito

A woman occasionally is quite a serviceable substitute for masturbation. It takes an abundance of imagination, to be sure.

Karl Kraus

Don't knock masturbation — it's sex with someone you love.

Woody Allen, in the film *Annie Hall*, 1977

DON'T DO THAT

On masturbation: It is called in our schools 'beastliness', and this is about the best name for it . . . Should it become a habit it quickly destroys both health and spirits; he becomes feeble in body and mind, and often ends in a lunatic asylum.

Sir Robert Baden-Powell, *Scouting for Boys,* 1908

Masturbation is great – and you don't have to take your hand out to dinner afterwards and talk to it about its problems.

Graffito

You know what I like about masturbation? You don't have to talk afterwards.

Milos Forman

The good thing about masturbation is that you don't have to dress up for it.

Truman Capote

One thing about masturbation – you don't have to look your best.

Graffito

Another thing about masturbation – you meet a better class of person.

Graffito

12

MARRIAGE IS AN INSTITUTION . . .

Young farmer with 100 acres would be pleased to hear from young lady with tractor. Please send photograph of tractor.

Advertisement in *Evesham Admag*, 1977

On marriage: The deep, deep peace of the double-bed after the hurly-burly of the chaise longue.

Mrs Patrick Campbell

If we take matrimony at its lowest, we regard it as a sort of friendship recognised by the police.

Robert Louis Stevenson

Courtship is to marriage as a very witty prologue is to a dull play.

William Congreve

I decided I had enjoyed myself long enough.

Princess Alice, Duchess of Gloucester, on her decision to accept the late Duke's marriage proposal

It begins with a prince kissing an angel. It ends with a baldheaded man looking across the table at a fat woman.

Anonymous

It begins when you sink into his arms; and ends with your arms in his sink.

Graffito

Marriage is a feast where the grace is sometimes better than the dinner.

Charles Caleb Colton

Marriage — a book of which the first chapter is written in poetry and the remaining chapters in prose.

Beverley Nichols

Marriage is a covered dish.

Swiss Proverb

Marriage is a wonderful invention. But, then again, so is the bicycle repair kit.

Billy Connolly

Marriage may be compared to a cage. The birds outside despair to get in and those within despair to get out.

Montaigne

Marriage: the state or condition of a community consisting of a master, a mistress, and two slaves, making, in all, two.

Ambrose Bierce

I think marriage is a very personal thing.

Victoria Principal, 1984

If they only married when they fell in love most people would die unwed.

Robert Louis Stevenson

Marriage is the alliance of two people, one of whom never remembers birthdays and the other never forgets them.

Ogden Nash

The particular charm of marriage is the duologue, the permanent conversation between two people who talk over everything and everyone till death breaks the record. It is this back-chat which, in the long run, makes a reciprocal equality more intoxicating than any form of servitude or domination.

Cyril Connolly, *The Unquiet Grave,* 1944

I believe marriages would in general be as happy, and often more so, if they were all made by the Lord Chancellor, upon a due consideration of the characters and circumstances, without the parties having any choice in the matter.

Dr Samuel Johnson, 22 March 1776

No man should marry until he has studied anatomy and dissected at least one woman.

P.B. Shelley

My son got his first acting part, playing a man who's been married for thirty years. I told him to stick at it and next time he'd get a speaking part.

Henry Fonda, 1978

The most happy marriage I can picture . . . would be the union of a deaf man to a blind woman.

Samuel Taylor Coleridge

Nearly all marriages, even happy ones, are mistakes: in the sense that almost certainly (in a more perfect world, or even with a little more care in this very imperfect one) both partners might have found more suitable mates. But the real soul-mate is the one you are actually married to.

J.R.R. Tolkien, in a letter to his son Michael, March 1941

The best of all possible marriages is a seesaw in which first one then the other partner is dominant.

Dr Joyce Brothers

Wives are young men's mistresses, companions for middle age, and old men's nurses.

Francis Bacon, *Of Marriage and Single Life,* 1625

Getting married is a serious matter for a girl; not getting married is even more serious.

Nicolas Bentley

Marriage is popular because it combines the maximum of temptation with the maximum of opportunity.

George Bernard Shaw

To have a woman to lye with when one pleases, without running any risk of the cursed expense of bastards . . . These are solid views of matrimony.

Robert Burns

A man marries to have a home, but also because he doesn't want to be bothered with sex and all that sort of thing.

W. Somerset Maugham

Every bride has to learn it's not her wedding but her mother's.

Luci Johnson Nugent, 1966

If it were not for the presents, an elopement would be preferable.

George Ade

When an old man marries a young wife, he grows younger —
but she gets older.

Jewish proverb

I have always thought that every woman should marry and no
man.

Benjamin Disraeli

If you marry you will regret it. If you do not marry, you will
also regret it.

Sören Kierkegaard

Greater luck hath no man than this, that he lay down his wife
at the right moment.

Samuel Butler

On a widower's re-marrying: Were he not to marry again, it
might be concluded that his first wife had given him a disgust
to marriage; but by taking a second wife he pays the highest
compliment to the first, by shewing that she made him so
happy as a married man that he wishes to be so a second time.

Dr Samuel Johnson, 30 September 1769

When two divorced people marry, four get into bed.

Jewish proverb

To marry a second time represents the triumph of hope over
experience.

Dr Samuel Johnson

A man and a woman marry because both of them don't know
what to do with themselves.

Anton Chekhov

On getting married: It's like signing a 356-page contract without knowing what's in it.

Mick Jagger

The surest way to be alone is to get married.
Gloria Steinem

If you're afraid of loneliness, don't marry.
Anton Chekhov

The greatest thing about marriage is that it enables one to be alone without feeling loneliness.
Gerald Brenan, *Thoughts in a Dry Season,* 1978

It is easier to be a lover than a husband, for the same reason that it is more difficult to show a ready wit all day long than to say a good thing occasionally.
Honoré de Balzac

Husbands are chiefly good lovers when they are betraying their wives.
Marilyn Monroe

I was married once – in San Francisco. I haven't seen her for many years. The great earthquake and fire of 1906 destroyed the marriage certificate. There's no legal proof. Which proves that earthquakes aren't all bad.
W.C. Fields

If I were married to a hogshead of claret, matrimony would make me hate it.
Sir John Vanbrugh, *The Provoked Wife*

Marriage: a ceremony in which rings are put on the finger of the lady and through the nose of the gentleman.
Herbert Spencer

Most men fall in love with a pretty face but find themselves bound for life to a hateful stranger, alternating endlessly between a workshop and a witch's kitchen.

Arthur Schopenhauer

Marriage is the only war where one sleeps with the enemy.

Mexican proverb

In marriage, as in war, it is permitted to take every advantage of the enemy.

Douglas Jerrold

Marriage is good for nothing but to make friends fall out.

Thomas Shadwell, *The Sullen Lovers*

Women are like elephants to me: I like to look at them, but I wouldn't want to own one.

W.C. Fields

My Lord [the first Earl of Sandwich] told me that among his father's many old sayings that he had writ in a book of his, this is one; that he that doth get a wench with child and marries her afterward, it is as if a man should shit in his hat and then clap it upon his head.

Samuel Pepys, in his diary, 7 October 1660

I've sometimes thought of marrying – and then I've thought again.

Noel Coward

All tragedies are finished by death,
All comedies are ended by a marriage.

Lord Byron

I had no need to marry. I had three pets at home which answered the same purpose as a husband. I have a dog which growls every morning, a parrot which swears all the afternoon, and a cat which comes home late at night.

Marie Correlli, quoted by Sir James Crichton in *What the Doctor Thought*

For a male and female to live continuously together is . . . biologically speaking, an extremely unnatural condition.

Robert Briffault, *Sin and Sex*

A man in love is incomplete until he has married. Then he's finished.

Zsa Zsa Gabor

Taking numbers into account, I should think more mental suffering has been undergone in the streets leading from St George's, Hanover Square, than in the condemned cells of Newgate.

Samuel Butler, *The Way of All Flesh,* 1903

Marriage is a great institution, but I'm not ready for an institution yet.

Mae West

Love-matches are made by people who are content, for a month of honey, to condemn themselves to a life of vinegar.

The Countess of Blessington

Advice to persons about to marry – don't.

Henry Mayhew, in *Punch,* 1845

Keep thy eyes wide open before marriage and half shut afterward.

Thomas Fuller, 1731

Men marry because they are tired, women because they are curious; both are disappointed.

Oscar Wilde

Dora and I are now married, but just as happy as we were before.

Bertrand Russell

Love is blind, but marriage restores its sight.

George Christoph Lichtenberg

Marriage is a mistake every man should make.

George Jessel

Praise a wife but remain a bachelor.

Italian proverb

They dream in marriage but in wedlock wake.

Alexander Pope

Strange to say what delight we married people have to see these poor fools decoyed into our condition.

Samuel Pepys

Marriage is not a word but a sentence.

Anonymous

A certain kind of talent is indispensable for people who would spend years together and not bore themselves to death.

Robert Louis Stevenson

The only really happy people are married women and single men.

H.L. Mencken

Greatest horror – dream I am married – wake up shrieking.

J.M. Barrie, in a notebook at the age of eighteen

It is so far from being natural for a man and woman to live in a state of marriage that we find all the motives which they have for remaining in that connection, and the restraints which civilised society imposes to prevent separation are hardly sufficient to keep them together.

Dr Samuel Johnson, 31 March 1772

I was born in 1896, and my parents were married in 1919.

J.R. Ackerley, *My Father and Myself,* 1968

On the birth of his second son: We have nearly got a full polo team now.

Prince Charles, 1984

On pregnancy: It's a very boring time. I am not particularly maternal – it's an occupational hazard of being a wife.

Princess Anne, in a TV interview, April 1981

The critical period in matrimony is breakfast time.

A.P. Herbert

Basically my wife was immature. I'd be at home in the bath and she'd come in and sink my boats.

Woody Allen

In some countries being president is just an honorary position – like being a husband in Hollywood.

Earl Wilson

The one advantage about marrying a princess – or someone from a royal family – is that they do know what happens.

Prince Charles

One wife at a time is enough for most people.

Mr Justice Smith, May 1979

The London season is entirely matrimonial; people are either hunting for husbands or hiding from them.

Oscar Wilde

I married the Duke for better, for worse, but not for lunch.

The Duchess of Windsor

When it was suggested to him that the marriage of Thomas and Jane Carlyle had been a mistake: I totally disagree with you. By any other arrangement, *four* people would have been unhappy instead of two.

Samuel Butler

When a man has married a wife he finds out whether Her knees and elbows are only glued together.

William Blake

It doesn't much signify whom one marries, for one is sure to find next morning that it was someone else.

Benjamin Franklin

13

A LITTLE BIT ON THE SIDE

So heavy is the chain of wedlock that it needs two to carry it, and sometimes three.

Alexandre Dumas (fils)

The first thrill of adultery is entering the house. Everything there has been paid for by the other man.

John Updike, 1985

I don't think there are any men who are faithful to their wives.

Jacqueline Kennedy Onassis

I don't know of any young man, black or white, who doesn't have a girl friend besides his wife. Some have four sneaking around.

Muhammad Ali

Adultery is a most conventional way to rise above the conventional.

Vladimir Nabokov, *Lectures on Literature,* 1980

These are just some of the joys of youth but, oh, for the joys of adultery.

Anonymous schoolgirl, writing an essay on 'the joys of youth'

I was told when a young man that the two occupational hazards of the Palace of Varieties [Westminster] were alcohol and adultery. 'The Lords,' [an old peer] said severely, 'has the cup for adultery' ... The hurroosh that follows the intermittent revelation of the sexual goings-on of an unlucky MP has convinced me that the only safe pleasure for a parliamentarian is a bag of boiled sweets.

Julian Critchley MP, in an article for the *Listener*, 10 June 1982

Adultery in your heart is committed not only when you look with excessive sexual desire at a woman who is not your wife, but also if you look in the same manner at your wife.

Pope John Paul II, 1980

I can't take dictation. I can't type. I can't even answer the phone.

Elizabeth Ray, the Washington 'secretary' of Congressman Wayne Hays, 1976

Next to the pleasure of taking a new mistress is that of being rid of an old one.

William Wycherley, *The Country Wife,* 1672

A mistress should be like a little country retreat near the town; not to dwell in constantly, but only for a night and away!

William Wycherley, *The Country Wife,* 1672

I need several mistresses. If I had only one, she'd be dead inside eight days.

Alexandre Dumas (père)

When you marry your mistress, you create a job vacancy.

Sir James Goldsmith

I've looked on a lot of women with lust. I've committed adultery in my heart many times. God recognises I will do this and forgives me.

Jimmy Carter, interviewed in *Playboy*, November 1976

He who enjoys a good neighbour, said the Greeks, has a precious possession. Same goes for the neighbour's wife.

Nicolas Bentley

For my part I keep the commandments, I love my neighbour as myself, and to avoid coveting my neighbour's wife I desire to be coveted by her; which you know is quite another thing.

William Congreve, 1700

We in the industry know that behind every successful screenwriter stands a woman. And behind her stands his wife.

Groucho Marx

When you have an affair with a married man, you hear a lot more about his wife than you do about yourself.

Sandra Hochman, *Walking Papers,* 1971

Nowadays all the married men live like bachelors, and all the bachelors live like married men.

Oscar Wilde

I know in my heart it's true: that bastard's f***ing his wife.

Shelley Winters, *Shelley . . . Also Known as Shirley,* 1980

I say I don't sleep with married men, but what I mean is that I don't sleep with happily married men.

Britt Ekland, 1980

'Come, Come,' said Tom's father, 'at your time of life,
There's no longer excuse for this playing the rake –
It is time you should think, boy, of taking a wife' –
'Why, so it is, father – whose wife shall I take?'

Thomas Moore, *A Joke Versified*

He didn't need to take a change of shoes; he can always wear hers; she has very big feet, you know.

Vivien Merchant, on her husband, Harold Pinter, when he left her for Lady Antonia Fraser, quoted in December 1975

On being asked, 'How many husbands have you had?' You mean, apart from my own?

Zsa Zsa Gabor

No matter how happily a woman may be married, it always pleases her to discover that there is a nice man who wishes she were not.

Anonymous

A lover teaches a wife all that her husband has concealed from her.

Honoré de Balzac, *The Physiology of Marriage,* 1829

The prerequisite for a good marriage is the licence to be unfaithful.

C.G. Jung

A man can have two, maybe three, love affairs while he's married. But three is the absolute maximum. After that you're cheating.

Yves Montand

A woman we love rarely satisfies all our needs, and we deceive her with a woman whom we do not love.

Marcel Proust

As I have promised to conceal nothing from you I shall confess to you ingenuously that I have here intimate relations with a married lady. You ought not to be too alarmed about it, for I protest to you that our commerce is purely corporal, and that the heart has no part in it. As you will judge by the description that I am going to give you of this person, she is an abandoned lady, who welcomes all comers, but who happily nevertheless behaves rather well. She is bizarre and uncertain to a supreme degree, now of a marvellous tranquillity, now wild as the devil. Our rendezvous are every morning at seven o'clock; I throw myself completely nude into her arms, even without a shirt, and as she is of an appalling size I have not the least difficulty in getting at her. With all that, she is of a temperament very cold. But what is singular in our relations is that I emerge from her arms with more vigour and energy than when I went into them, which is good fortune rarely encountered. Finally you can conclude that I do not love her, and proof of that is that I shall tell you who she is. She is the Sea, the wife of Monsieur the Doge of Venice, and I hope that he and you will both pardon me this affair.

The 4th Earl of Chesterfield

When his wife caught him kissing a chorus-girl: I wasn't kissing her. I was whispering in her mouth.

Chico Marx

Open marriage is nature's way of telling you you need a divorce.

Marshall Brickman

In married life, three is company and two none.

Oscar Wilde

14

A VERY LOVING SEPARATION

Love, the quest; marriage, the conquest; divorce, the inquest.
  Helen Rowland

Divorces are made in heaven.
  Oscar Wilde

You never really know a man until you have divorced him.
  Zsa Zsa Gabor

The happiest time of anyone's life is just after the first divorce.
  John Kenneth Galbraith

When his wife abandoned him: I did not forsake her, I did not dismiss her: I will not recall her.
  John Wesley

To Lord Snowdon on the break-up of his marriage to Princess Margaret: Your experience will be a lesson to all of us men to be careful not to marry ladies in very high positions.
  Idi Amin, March 1976

The only solid and lasting peace between a man and his wife is doubtless a separation.
  The 4th Earl of Chesterfield

My wife got the house, the car, the bank account, and if I marry again and have children, she gets them too.

Woody Allen

It was partially my fault we got divorced. I had a tendency to place my wife under a pedestal.

Woody Allen

On having a 'very loving separation' from her husband: We're going to rotate the house and we even rotate the car. We've been separated for four months and it's a growing experience.
Talia Shire

Many a man owes his success to his first wife, and his second wife to his success.
Jim Backus

Asking for a daughter's hand in marriage: As you know I'm in show business, so could I ask if she could be my *first* wife.
Anonymous

Alimony is like buying oats for a dead horse.
Arthur Baer

Alimony is the screwing you get for the screwing you got.
Graffito

I am a marvellous housekeeper. Every time I leave a man, I keep his house.
Zsa Zsa Gabor

The difference between divorce and legal separation is that a legal separation gives a husband time to hide his money.
Johnny Carson

Husbands are like fires. They go out when unattended.
Zsa Zsa Gabor

It takes two to destroy a marriage.
Margaret Trudeau

Why is it that when married couples separate, they so often tend to blame each other for the very qualities that attracted them to each other in the first place?

Sydney J. Harris

15

ON THE PAGE, ON THE STAGE, AND ON THE SCREEN

Nudge nudge, wink wink. Say no more. Know what I mean?

Eric Idle, as the prurient character in *Monty Python's Flying Circus*

On the book 'Lady Chatterley's Lover' by D.H. Lawrence: Is it a book that you would have lying around in your own house? Is this a book that you would ever wish your wife or your servants to read?

Mervyn Griffith Jones, prosecuting counsel at the trial of the book's publishers on obscenity charges, 1961

I shall not say why and how I became, at the age of 15, the mistress of the Earl of Craven.

Harriet Wilson, *Memoirs of Herself and Others*

I don't see so much of Alfred at night any more since he got so interested in sex.

Mrs Alfred Kinsey, wife of the author of the *Kinsey Report on Sexual Behaviour*

Chaste men engender obscene literatures.

Ausonius

I had cherished a profound conviction that her bringing me up by hand gave her no right to bring me up by jerks.

Charles Dickens, *Great Expectations*

Meredith had an unbounded enthusiasm for French letters.

Anonymous editor of George Meredith's letters to Alice Meynell

On 'Oh, Calcutta!': This is the kind of show that gives pornography a bad name.

Clive Barnes, 1969

On the opening night of 'Oh, Calcutta!': The trouble with nude dancing is that not everything stops when the music stops.

Sir Robert Helpmann

To David Garrick: I'll come no more behind your scenes, David; for the silk stockings and white bosoms of your actresses excite my amorous propensities.

Samuel Johnson

You know, I go to the theatre to be entertained . . . I don't want to see plays about rape, sodomy and drug addiction . . . I can get all that at home.

Peter Cook, cartoon caption in the *Observer,* 8 July 1962

When asked if she had really posed for a calendar with nothing on: Oh no, I had the radio on.

Marilyn Monroe

On topless models: They're going to turn us all off sex pretty soon if they don't stop.

Jane Russell, 1986

The words 'Kiss Kiss Bang Bang' which I saw on an Italian movie poster are perhaps the briefest statement imaginable on the basic appeal of movies.

Pauline Kael, *Kiss Kiss Bang Bang,* 1968

The artist has won through his fantasy what before he could only win *in* his fantasy: honour, power, and the love of women.

Sigmund Freud, *Introductory Lectures in Psycho-Analysis, No 23,* 1916

Sex perversion or any inference of it is forbidden . . . sex hygiene and venereal diseases are not subjects for motion pictures. Scenes of actual childbirth, in fact or in silhouette, are never to be represented. Children's sex organs are never to be exposed.

A Code to Govern the Making of Motion and Talking Pictures by the Motion Picture Producers and Distributors of America, Inc., 1930

The sanctity of the institution of marriage and the home shall be upheld. Pictures shall not infer that low forms of sex relationship are the accepted or common thing.

A Code to Govern etc.

Discussing a film documentary about the South Seas: Boys, I've got an idea. Let's fill the whole screen with tits.

Hunt Stromberg

Listen, who do I have to f*** to get *off* this picture?

Terry Southern, *Blue Movie,* 1970

My music isn't supposed to make you wanna riot. My music is supposed to make you wanna f***!

Janis Joplin

16

PARTICULAR MEN

When told that Lord Astor had denied any involvement with her:
Well, he would, wouldn't he?

Mandy Rice-Davies, 1963

On Gary Cooper: He was hung like a horse and he could go all night.

Clara Bow

I would rather go to bed with a cold cod than the Hon. Member for Perth and Kinross [Nicholas Fairbairn].

Janet Fookes MP, 1985

The trouble with Ian [Fleming] is that he gets off with women because he can't get on with them.

Rosamond Lehmann, borrowing a line from Elizabeth Bowen and quoted in John Pearson's *The Life of Ian Fleming*

Hearst come, Hearst served.

Marion Davies, mistress of William Randolph Hearst

To Harold Macmillan: If I go too long without a woman, I suffer severe headaches.

John F. Kennedy

No one was off-limits with Jack [Kennedy] — not your wife, your mother, your sister.

Senator George Smathers

I'm never through with a girl until I've had her three ways.

John F. Kennedy

On Henry Kissinger: Henry's idea of sex is to slow down to thirty miles an hour when he drops you off at the door.

Barbara Howar

When the Earl of Lichfield said he was dropping her because 'she was no good in the country': And he's no good in bed.

Britt Ekland

There are three things that my brother Chico is always on: a phone, a horse, or a broad.

Groucho Marx

They say a man is as old as the woman he feels. In that case I'm eighty-five.

Groucho Marx

Dudley Moore is a phallic thimble.

Graffito

He kept telling me he was a confirmed bachelor and I thought at least one knows where one stands.

Princess Anne, on Captain Mark Phillips, November 1973

My saddler told me, [John Selden, lawyer] got more by his prick than by his practice.

John Aubrey, *Brief Lives*

I love Mickey Mouse more than any woman I've ever known.
Walt Disney

After her first night with Orson Welles: I looked at his head on the pillow and knew that he was just waiting for the applause.

Rita Hayworth

He had one arm round your waist and one eye on the clock.

Margot Asquith

On a small, potential lover: The problem was that when I was young I used to like to do it standing up and, if I had ever done it with him, he would have been jabbing me in the knees.

Josephine Baker

Photo inscription to her fiancé: To my gorgeous lover, Harry. I'll trade all my It for your that.

Clara Bow, the 'It' Girl

On the Mormon ex-lover she had kidnapped and chained to the bed: I loved Kirk so much, I would have skied down Mount Everest in the nude with a carnation up my nose.

Joyce McKinney, in an English court, 1977

17

PARTICULAR WOMEN

On Edwina Currie MP: All the poison that my Hon. Friend suggested I would happily take rather than be spreadeagled on the floor of the House by her.

Nicholas Fairbairn MP, in the House of Commons, January 1985

Romance on the High Seas was Doris Day's first picture; that was before she became a virgin.

Oscar Levant, *Memoirs of an Amnesiac,* 1965

On Florence Day, the actress and variety artiste: Little Day, you've had a busy man.

Bud Flanagan

On Britt Ekland: She's a professional girl-friend and an amateur actress.

Peter Sellers

To Clive James: I'm sorry, I only sleep with the first eleven.

Lady Antonia Fraser (attrib.)

Explaining why he was sacked from the government: It is shapely, it wiggles, and its name is Ainslie Gotto.

Dudley Erwin, Australian air minister, 1969 (Ms Gotto was the Prime Minister's secretary)

Of the Empress Josephine: Far-sighted nature had placed the wherewithal to pay her bills beneath her navel.

Anonymous

When Kitty (Jean Harlow) mentions that 'machinery is going to take the place of every profession': That's something you need never worry about.

Marie Dressler, as 'Carlotta' in the film *Dinner at Eight,* 1933

Linda Lovelace went down in my estimation.

Graffito

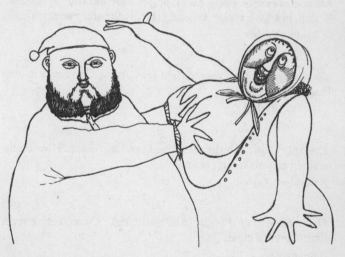

By her breasts she should be no maid; which, when I felt them, strake me so to the heart that I had neither will nor courage to prove the rest.

King Henry VIII (to Thomas Cromwell), after his wedding night with Anne of Cleves, his fourth wife.

On signing her first big film contract: That's the last cock I'll have to suck.

Marilyn Monroe

Marilyn Monroe? A vacuum with nipples.

Otto Preminger

When Eva Peron complained to him that she had been called a whore during a visit to Italy: Quite so. But I have not been on a ship for fifteen years and they still call me 'Admiral'.

Anonymous Italian official

On a Hallowe'en party where people were ducking for apples: There, but for a typographical error, is the story of my life.

Dorothy Parker

When pregnant: It serves me right for putting all my eggs in one bastard.

Dorothy Parker

I've only slept with the men I've been married to. How many women can make that claim?

Elizabeth Taylor

Of the Duchess of Windsor: She could make a match-stick seem like a Havana cigar.

Anonymous

On an available Nordic blonde: Ah, I see the Danish open sandwich is with us again.

Anonymous

That woman speaks eighteen languages, and she can't say 'no' in any of them.

Dorothy Parker

She wears her c*** on her sleeve.

Anonymous

Suggested epitaph for an available actress: She sleeps alone at last.

Robert Benchley

Of an available starlet: She was the original good time that was had by all.

Bette Davis

Barbara Stanwyck is my favourite. My God, I could just sit and dream of being married to her, having a little cottage out in the hills, vines around the door. I'd come home from the office, tired, weary, and I'd be met by Barbara, walking through the door holding an apple that she had cooked herself. And wearing no drawers.

Herman J. Mankiewicz

18
THERE'S A LOT OF PROMISCUITY ABOUT

There's a lot of promiscuity about these days, and I'm all for it.
Ben Travers (aged 94), 1980

What is a promiscuous person? It's usually someone who is getting more sex than you are.
Victor Lownes

If all the young girls at the Yale Prom were laid end to end, I wouldn't be at all surprised.
Dorothy Parker

It's one thing to f*** someone you don't know and another thing to look at him over coffee in the morning.
Judith Rossner, *Looking for Mr Goodbar,* 1975

Save a boyfriend for a rainy day and another in case it doesn't.
Mae West

I don't want to see any faces at this party that I haven't sat on.
Anonymous Hollywood actress

It's impossible to ravish me I'm so willing.
John Fletcher, *The Faithful Shepherdess,* 1610

I like to wake up feeling a new man.

Jean Harlow

Cannes is where you lie on the beach and look at the stars – or vice versa.

Rex Reed

Our world has changed. It's no longer a question of 'Does she or doesn't she?' We all know she wants to, is about to, or does.

'J', in *The Sensuous Woman*

The orgasm has replaced the Cross as the focus of longing and the image of fulfilment.

Malcolm Muggeridge, 'Down with Sex', *Tread Softly for You Tread on My Jokes*, 1966

Chivalry: going about releasing beautiful maidens from other men's castles, and taking them to your own castle.

Henry W. Nevinson

On seeing two musicians affected by drugs: I don't understand it. I'm a c*** man myself.

Duke Ellington

This administration is going to do for sex what the last one [Eisenhower's] did for golf.

Anonymous aide to John F. Kennedy

If you aren't going all the way, why go at all?

Joe Namath

A vasectomy means never having to say you're sorry.

Anonymous

Dudes always used to tell that lie: 'I can f*** eight, nine hours, Jack.' You're a lyin' motherf***er. I can do about three minutes of serious f***in', and then I need about eight hours sleep, and a bowl of Wheaties.

Richard Pryor, *Live in Concert,* 1979

On a stag party: Anyone who could stick a cock in one of those girls would throw a rock through a Rembrandt.

Humphrey Bogart

I do a lot of research, especially in the apartments of tall blondes.

Raymond Chandler

Outside every thin girl there is a fat man trying to get in.

Katharine Whitehorn

19

UNUSUAL, TO SAY THE LEAST

While the hopeless ecstasy of his huge pent-up spasm began
. . . sweet Candy's melodious voice rang out through the
temple in truly mixed feelings: 'GOOD GRIEF–IT'S
DADDY!'

Terry Southern and Maxwell Hoffenberg, *Candy,* 1958

What is wrong with a little incest? It is both handy and cheap.

James Agate

The trouble with incest is that it gets you involved with
relatives.

George S. Kaufman

I have never been able to understand how a father could
tenderly love his charming daughter without having slept with
her at least once.

Giovanni Jacopo Casanova

You should make a point of trying every experience once –
except incest and folk dancing.

Anonymous Scotsman, quoted by Sir Arnold Bax in *Farewell to My
Youth,* 1943

I am fond of children (except boys).

Revd C.L. Dodgson (Lewis Carroll)

Buggery is boring.
Incest is relatively boring.
Necrophilia is dead boring.

Graffito

I was a beautiful little boy, and everyone had me – men, women, dogs and fire hydrants.

Truman Capote

I swallow well.

Linda Lovelace

Never do with your hands what you could do better with your mouth.

Cherry Vanilla, groupie

She's going to get me some work – a blow job.

Steve Martin, in his film *The Jerk,* 1979

I regret to say that we of the FBI are powerless to act in cases of oral-genital intimacy, unless it has in some way obstructed interstate commerce.

J. Edgar Hoover

Personally I have always felt [*soixante-neuf*] to be madly confusing, like trying to pat your head and rub your stomach at the same time.

Helen Lawrenson

There is no more lively sensation than that of pain.

Marquis de Sade

Sado-masochism means not having to say you are sorry.

Graffito

I'm all for bringing back the birch, but only between consenting adults.

Gore Vidal

There's nothing wrong with going to bed with somebody of your own sex . . . People should be very free with sex — they should draw the line at goats.

Elton John

Sex between a man and a woman can be wonderful – provided you get between the right man and the right woman.

Woody Allen

On a famous pair about to get married: Splendid couple – slept with both of them.

Sir Maurice Bowra

He was into animal husbandry – until they caught him at it.

Tom Lehrer

Among the porcupines, rape is unknown.

Gregory Clark

There is no unhappier creature on earth than a fetishist who yearns for a woman's shoes and has to embrace the whole woman.

Karl Kraus, *Aphorisms and More Aphorisms,* 1909

Certainly nothing is unnatural that is not physically impossible.

Richard Brinsley Sheridan, *The Critic,* 1779

Some things can't be ravished. You can't ravish a tin of sardines.

D.H. Lawrence, *Lady Chatterley's Lover*

20

I CAN'T GET NO . . .

To Bernard Shaw, after an empty flirtation: You had no right to write the preface if you were not going to write the book.
  Edith Nesbit

Nothing is so much to be shunned as sexual relations.
  St Augustine, *Soliloquies*

The expense of spirit in a waste of shame
Is lust in action . . .
Enjoy'd no sooner but despised straight . . .
Before, a joy propos'd; behind, a dream.
  William Shakespeare, Sonnet 129

All this fuss about sleeping together. For physical pleasure I'd sooner go to my dentist any day.
  Evelyn Waugh, *Vile Bodies,* 1930

Sex is a bad thing because it rumples the clothes.
  Jacqueline Kennedy Onassis

A man has missed something if he has never woken up in an anonymous bed beside a face he'll never see again, and if he has never left a brothel at dawn feeling like jumping off a bridge into the river out of sheer physical disgust with life.
  Gustave Flaubert

Niagara is only the second biggest disappointment of the standard honeymoon.

Oscar Wilde

I'm afraid Mr Mouse didn't come out to play.

The 10th Duke of Marlborough, on returning from one of his honeymoons

The first time is never the best.

Advertising slogan for Campari

They say a woman should be a cook in the kitchen and a whore in bed. Unfortunately, my wife is a whore in the kitchen and a cook in bed.

Anonymous

On Maureen O'Hara: She looked as though butter wouldn't melt in her mouth — or anywhere else.

Elsa Lanchester

A man who exposes himself when he is intoxicated has not the art of getting drunk.

Dr Samuel Johnson

Mummy, mummy, what's an orgasm? — I dunno. Ask your father.

Graffito

Friday night too tired, Saturday night too drunk, Sunday night too far away.

Anonymous Australian sheep shearer's wife

On drink and sex: Lechery, sir, it provokes and unprovokes: it provokes the desire, but it takes away the performance. Therefore, much drink may be said to be an equivocator with lechery; it makes him, and it mars him; it sets him on, and it takes him off; it persuades him, and disheartens him; makes him stand to, and not stand to; in conclusion, equivocates him in a sleep, and, giving him the lie, leaves him.

William Shakespeare, *Macbeth* (the Porter), 1605

Onstage I make love to twenty-five thousand people, then I go home alone.

Janis Joplin

I'm a big star and I can't even get laid.

Janis Joplin

Take me or leave me.
Or as most people do: both.

Dorothy Parker

When my bed is empty,
Makes me feel awful mean and blue.
My springs are getting rusty,
Living single like I do.

Bessie Smith, 'Empty Bed Blues', *c.* 1928

After being on the receiving end of a strong handshake: Thank you. That's the nearest thing to sex I've had all day.

Anonymous

21

AFTER-WORDS

Good girls go to heaven, bad girls go everywhere.

Helen Gurley-Brown, promotional line for *Cosmopolitan* magazine

When I'm good, I'm very good. When I'm bad, I'm better.

Mae West

Thanks, I enjoyed every inch of it.

Mae West

I used to be Snow White but I drifted.

Mae West

I have been one of the great lovers of my century.

Sarah Bernhardt

My mother said it was simple to keep a man, you must be a maid in the living room, a cook in the kitchen and a whore in the bedroom. I said I'd hire the other two and take care of the bedroom bit.

Jerry Hall, 1985

There comes a point where every woman has to face up to being an old broad.

Ava Gardner, 1984

Is it not strange that desire should so many years outlive performance.

William Shakespeare, *King Henry IV, Part II*

Show me a naked girl and I'll show you how quickly I can go to sleep.

Groucho Marx (in old age, although he had advised reporters that his relationship with his secretary was 'purely physical')

When asked towards the end of his life whether he had any regrets:
Yes, I haven't had enough sex.

Sir John Betjeman, in the TV programme *Time With Betjeman,* February 1983

Delighted you came, my dear, and I'd like you to know that you made a happy man feel very old.

Terry-Thomas, in the film *The Last Remake of Beau Geste,* 1977

She offered her honour,
I honoured her offer,
So all night long
It was on her and off her.

Anonymous

Boy, am I exhausted! I went on a double date last night and the other girl didn't show up.

Mae West

On being offered oysters in the 1880s: I don't need these adventitious aids. Lady Parkes and I until quite recently have been in the habit of having connection 17 or 18 times every night, and we now have connection 10 or 11 times.

Sir Henry Parkes, Australian politician

I've been to bed with no less than one thousand women in my life.

Elvis Presley

I have made love to ten thousand women.

Georges Simenon, interviewed in *Die Tat*, 1977 (Later, his wife said, 'The true figure is no more than twelve hundred')

My own wife, as some people know, had a lot of children — eight if I remember rightly.

The 7th Earl of Longford, 1985

We have been on a working honeymoon.

David Frost, 1983

Making small-talk with David Frost: Well, did you do any fornicating this weekend?

Richard Nixon, 1977

Fornication: but that was in another country:
And beside the wench is dead.

Christopher Marlowe, *The Jew of Malta*

Male inquiry after intercourse: Did thee feel the earth move?

Ernest Hemingway, *For Whom the Bell Tolls*, 1940 (She replies, 'Yes')

Oh! joy it was for her, and joy for me!

William Wordsworth

In response to a striking miner's observation. 'Hey, love, your horse is foaming at the mouth': I'm not surprised; so would you be if you'd been between my legs for the last two hours.

Anonymous mounted policewoman, quoted in 1984

When her lover, the Prince of Wales (later King Edward VII), complained, 'I've spent enough on you to buy a battleship': And you've spent enough in me to float one.

Lillie Langtry

Never sleep with a woman whose troubles are worse than your own.

Nelson Algren, *A Walk on the Wild Side*, 1956

When a woman tells him, 'You are the greatest lover I have ever known': Well, I practise a lot when I'm on my own.

Woody Allen, in the film *Love and Death*, 1975

Tell him I've been too f***ing busy – or vice versa.

Dorothy Parker

Making love, ends meet, and people laugh.

Nicholas Fairbairn MP, listing his hobbies in *Who's Who,* 1973

Bunking and debunking.

Nicholas Fairbairn MP, listing his hobbies in *Who's Who,* 1977

When chided on the size of his stomach by Lady Astor with the words, 'What would you say if that was on a woman?': Madam, half an hour ago it was.

Lord Castlerosse

On double beds v. single beds: It is not the wild, ecstatic leap across that I deplore. It is the weary trudge home.

Anonymous.

INDEX OF PEOPLE QUOTED

Barrie, J.M. 72
Barrymore, John 15, 38
Beatty, Warren 22, 30
Beecham, Sir Thomas 30
Behan, Brendan 54
Bellow, Saul 45
Belushi, John 14
Benchley, Robert 97
Bennett, Arnold 9
Bentley, Nicolas 65, 78
Berg, Tonia 16
Bernard, Jeffrey 37
Berners, Lord 27
Bernhardt, Sarah 109
Betjeman, Sir John 110
Bible 22
Bierce, Ambrose 63
Bismarck, Prince Otto von 29
Blake, William 74
Blessington, Countess of 70
Bogart, Humphrey 100
Bow, Clara 90, 93
Bowra, Sir Maurice 104
Braun, Eva 57
Brenan, Gerald 68
Brickman, Marshall 81
Briffault, Robert 70
Brothers, Dr Joyce 65
Bryant, Anita 26
Burns, Robert 45, 65
Burton, Sir Richard 29
Butler, Montagu 17
Butler, Samuel 22, 31, 35, 66, 70, 74
Butz, Earl 53
Byrd, William 56
Byron, Lord 43, 69

Friedman, Robert 40
Frost, David 44, 111
Fuller, Thomas 70

Gabor, Zsa Zsa 17, 35, 70, 80, 82,
    84 (2)
Galbraith, J.K. 82
Gardner, Ava 109
George, Boy 15
Gershwin, George 41
Goethe, Wolfgang von 22
Goldsmith, Sir James 76
Gourmont, Rémy de 20
Gowrie, Earl of 46
Graham, Sheila 57
Grant, Cary 9
Greer, Germaine 15, 16
Gurley-Brown, Helen 109

Hall, Jerry 109
Hampton, Christopher 59
Hardy, Thomas 10
Harlow, Jean 13, 49, 99
Harris, Sydney J. 85
Hawker, Col. Peter 46
Hawn, Goldie 58
Hayworth, Rita 93
Helpmann, Sir Robert 87
Hemingway, Ernest 12, 111
Henry VIII, King 95
Herbert, A.P. 72
Hibberd, Jack 45
Hillingdon, Alice Lady 53
Hitchcock, Joan 17
Hochman, Sandra 78
Hoffenberg, Maxwell 101
Hoffman, Ward 30

Lerner, Alan Jay 31
Levant, Oscar 94
Levin, Bernard 19
Lichtenberg, G.C. 71
Longford, 7th Earl of 111
Loren, Sophia 44
Lovelace, Linda 102
Lownes, Victor 98
Lowry, L.S. 22
Luce, Clare Boothe 20
Lynch, Jack 53

McKinney, Joyce 93
MacLaine, Shirley 48
Mankiewicz, Herman J. 97
Mansfield, Jayne 11, 57
Marlborough, 10th Duke of 106
Marlborough, Sarah Duchess of 53
Marlowe, Christopher 111
Martin, Steve 102
Marx, Chico 81
Marx, Groucho 9, 11, 28, 78, 91 (2),
    110
Masson, Thomas L. 40
Mastroianni, Marcello 42
Maugham, W. Somerset 41, 65
Mayhew, Henry 70
Mencken, H.L. 22, 30, 35, 39, 71
Merchant, Vivienne 79
Mikes, George 42
Miller, Karl 54
Mizner, Wilson 9
Monroe, Marilyn 68, 87, 96
Montaigne 63
Montand, Yves 80
Montefiore, Revd Hugh 25
Montgomery, Viscount 25

Pryor, Richard 100
Pushkin, Alexander S. 40

Rachel, Mlle 14
Ray, Elizabeth 76
Reagan, Ronald 55
Reed, Rex 99
Rice-Davies, Mandy 90
Robertson, Sir John 52
Rossner, Judith 98
Rotten, Johnny 54
Rowland, Helen 24 (2), 82
Rubinstein, Artur 19
Rubirosa, Porfirio 19
Russell, Bertrand 17, 39, 71
Russell, Jane 87

Sade, Marquis de 102
Sagan, Françoise 33, 39, 49, 52
Sahl, Mort 28
Sassoon, Vidal 45
Savalas, Telly 45
Schopenhauer, Arthur 30, 69
Seaman, Barbara 14
Segal, Erich 39
Sellers, Peter 94
Sévigné, Mme. de 33
Shakespeare, William 105, 107, 110
Shadwell, Thomas 69
Shaw, George Bernard 47, 65
Shelley, Percy Bysshe 64
Sheridan, Richard Brinsley 104
Shields, Brooke 47
Shire, Talia 84
Simenon, Georges 111
Sloane, Everett 10
Smathers, George 90

Waugh, Evelyn 105
Welles, Orson 34
Wesley, John 82
West, Mae 12, 13, 14 (2), 22, 35 (2),
    41, 43, 49, 54, 58, 70, 98, 109 (3),
    110
Whitehorn, Katharine 100
Whitelaw, William 12
Wilde, Oscar 22, 23, 40, 41, 71, 74,
    78, 81, 82, 106
Wilson, Earl 72
Wilson, Harriet 86
Windsor, Duchess of 74
Winters, Shelley 78
Wodehouse, P.G. 49
Wordsworth, William 111
Wyatt, Woodrow 44
Wycherley, William 76 (2)

ENVOI

In response to a man's statement, 'I'd like to make love to you':
Well, if you do, and I ever get to hear about it, I shall be very
cross indeed.

Anonymous female journalist, quoted 1984